Wage I

International Comparisons of Its Sources

Francine D. Blau and Lawrence M. Kahn

The AEI Press

Publisher for the American Enterprise Institute

WASHINGTON, D.C.

1996

We are grateful to David Blanchflower, Per-Anders Edin, and Andrea Ichino for their help in acquiring data. Portions of this work were completed while we were visiting fellows at the Australian National University, Canberra. We have benefited from the helpful comments of Robert Topel and participants at workshops at the University of Illinois, Cornell University, University of Chicago, University of Oregon, Columbia University, University of Washington, Seattle, Washington State University, Pullman, and Georgia State University. We also thank those who attended presentations at the American Enterprise Institute, the 1994 NBER Summer Institute, the 1995 American Economic Association Meetings, and the INSEE Conference in Paris, France, 1996, for their suggestions.

Available in the United States from the AEI Press, c/o Publisher Resources Inc., 1224 Heil Quaker Blvd., P.O. Box 7001, La Vergne, TN 37086-7001. Distributed outside the United States by arrangement with Eurospan, 3 Henrietta Street, London WC2E 8LU England.

ISBN 0-8447-7074-4

1   3   5   7   9   10   8   6   4   2

THE AEI PRESS
Publisher for the American Enterprise Institute
1150 17th Street, N.W., Washington, D.C. 20036

Printed in the United States of America

Contents

Foreword

This study is one of a series commissioned by the American Enterprise Institute on trends in the level and distribution of U.S. wages, income, wealth, consumption, and other measures of material welfare. The issues addressed in the series involve much more than dry statistics: they touch on fundamental aspirations of the American people—material progress, widely shared prosperity, and just reward for individual effort—and affect popular understanding of the successes and shortcomings of the private market economy and of particular government policies. For these reasons, discussions of "economic inequality" in the media and political debate are often partial and partisan as well as superficial. The AEI series is intended to improve the public discussion by bringing new data to light, by exploring the strengths and weaknesses of various measures of economic welfare, and by highlighting important questions of interpretations, causation, and consequence.

Each study in the series is presented and discussed in draft form at an AEI seminar prior to revision by the author and publication by the AEI Press. Marvin Kosters, director of economic policy studies at AEI, directed the series and moderated the seminars. A current list of published studies appears on the last page.

CHRISTOPHER DEMUTH
President, American Enterprise Institute

Wage Inequality

T he level of wage inequality generated by a country's labor market is of fundamental importance for those interested in understanding poverty, social stratification, and the economic incentives facing workers. Labor earnings are by far the most significant component of income for individuals who are employed. Hence, in the absence of any compensatory government policies, low living standards in market economies will be associated with low labor incomes.[1] More generally, labor market inequality is a major determinant of disparities in living standards.

This study explores and seeks to explain an important phenomenon: namely, that wages are more unequal in the United States than they are in other advanced industrial economies. That is, the gap is larger in the United States between low wages at the bottom of the wage distribution and high wages at the top. This is a fact of international life. It has been well established by a number of studies and is not in dispute.

An equally important fact is less well known, however, and we will also explore *its* implications and

This study draws on our longer paper, "International Differences in Male Wage Inequality: Institutions versus Market Forces," *Journal of Political Economy*, vol. 104 (August 1996): 791–837.

causes. This second fact can be illustrated by a hypothetical example, comparing the United States with another typical industrial country. It should be remembered that, apart from the issue of inequality, wages in the United States are generally a little higher than they are abroad. Let us say, for purposes of this example, that the top wage in the United States is $100 an hour and the top wage in country X is $90 an hour; the bottom wage in the United States is $5 an hour and in country X it is $9. Clearly the larger wage gap is in the United States.

Now let us look further, breaking categories of wage earners into percentiles. Suppose that the middle wage group in the United States—the fiftieth percentile—earns $20 an hour; in country X, this group earns $18 an hour. This means that half of all the workers in the United States earn $20 an hour or more, and the other half earn less than $20 an hour; likewise, in country X, half of the workers earn $18 an hour or more, and the other half earn less than $18 an hour. Note that the gap between the top wage and the middle wage is the same in both countries—with the top wage five times the middle wage. *The entire difference in the total wage gap between the top and the bottom is accounted for by the much bigger difference in the United States between the fiftieth percentile and the bottom.* In the United States, the median wage is four times the bottom wage, whereas in country X it is only twice the bottom wage. Put another way, there is much more wage "compression" in country X at the bottom end of the distribution.

Although this example is hypothetical, it illustrates a real point, as shown by data presented later in this study. The wage gap—the inequality issue—is not as simple as it may appear at first glance.

There are both favorable and unfavorable aspects to wage compression at the bottom of the distribution.

To the extent that labor market inequality reflects economic returns to skills, international differences in inequality imply differences in incentives. Countries with high rewards for skills have a wage structure that encourages the acquisition of skills by their workers. This important positive factor for productivity is less powerfully at work in countries with more wage compression. Moreover, centralized wage-setting mechanisms that reduce wage variation tend to limit firms' flexibility in responding to differences in labor market conditions across industries or geographical areas. Also of concern, relatively high wages for low-skill groups may reduce the relative employment of these workers. This effect has been the subject of much recent research.[2]

An unfavorable aspect of high rewards for labor market skills, however, is that less-skilled workers are more likely to experience poverty or very low incomes. In addition, high rewards for labor market skills penalize demographic groups with below-average levels of skill, even in the absence of explicit discrimination. The rising returns to skill in the United States in the 1980s, for example, have been found to reduce the relative wages of black workers and immigrants and to retard the economic progress of women. Similarly, the authors found in a recent series of studies that the higher rewards to skills and high returns to employment in favored sectors in the United States, compared with those in other industrialized countries, were the most significant reason for the relatively large gender pay gap in the United States.[3]

Considerable attention has been focused lately on the trend in most of the industrialized countries toward rising wage inequality.[4] Evidence that inequality increased in countries with different institutional structures suggests that similar forces have been at work around the globe. It has been suggested, for example, that technological change and freer international trade have raised the relative demand for skilled workers among industrialized nations and widened the pay gap.

While changes in the demand for skilled labor appear to have led to a widening of wage inequality in many countries during the 1980s, considerable differences in the *level*, or degree, of inequality remain. Of particular interest, the United States still has a far greater dispersion of wages than do other industrialized countries, even though the level of inequality in these other countries has also increased somewhat. Previous international comparative work on wage inequality has focused on recent changes in wage dispersion. In this study we are concerned with understanding the fundamental causes of the higher *level* of wage inequality in the United States compared with the level in other industrialized countries in the 1980s. We concentrate on males as a relatively homogeneous sample of workers for each country.[5]

Figure 1 illustrates the basic pattern of international differences in wage inequality that we seek to explain. We use the logarithm of wages rather than the wages themselves, because this technique transforms wage differences (for example, those in dollars) into approximate percentage differences, facilitating cross-country comparisons. As expected on the basis of previous work, the United States has a considerably higher level of wage inequality than do the other industrial countries in our sample.

Panels A and B indicate that the standard deviation of log wages and the 90–10 percentile log wage differential are both considerably greater in the United States than in the other countries. Panel B indicates that in the United States, someone at the ninetieth percentile earns five times as much as someone at the tenth percentile, whereas in the next closest country,

Britain, the ratio is three and one-half times. The average of all the other countries in our sample is 2.7.

Panels C and D support the key point made in the hypothetical example given at the beginning of this study: that is, the higher level of inequality in the United States reflects considerably more compression at the bottom of the distribution in the other countries relative to the United States, but a much smaller difference in the degree of wage inequality at the top of the distribution. In panel D, showing the 90–50 differential, or the "gap at the top," the United States is about average, although panel C, on the 50–10 gap, shows the United States far ahead of the field.

Published data show a pattern similar to that revealed in our microdata. Specifically, the OECD (1993) surveyed wage inequality in its member countries and found that the 50–10 gap was far larger in the United States than in other countries. Although the 90–50 gap was also larger in the United States, the difference between the 90–50 gap in the United States and that of other countries was much smaller than the corresponding difference for the 50–10 gap.[6]

This pattern of greater compression at the bottom is important from a policy perspective, because it implies that the labor market reward structure in other countries generates less poverty and relatively higher incomes for employed low-skill workers than are generated in the United States.[7] Of course, as suggested above, the potential costs of wage compression would have to be compared with these benefits in assessing the desirability of this situation.

In what follows, we focus on three possible explanations for these international differences in patterns of wage inequality. We examine the role of differences across countries in the distribution of measured characteristics of the labor force. These characteristics include, for example, education levels, occupations, work

FIGURE 1
SUMMARY MEASURES OF WAGE INEQUALITY AMONG MALES IN SELECTED OECD COUNTRIES, 1985–1989

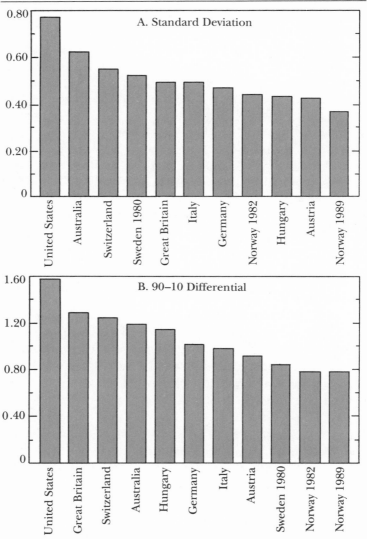

NOTES: For details of the construction of the wage measures, see the text of this study. As indicated above, data for Sweden and for one of our Norwegian data sets are for the early 1980s.

FIGURE 1 (continued)

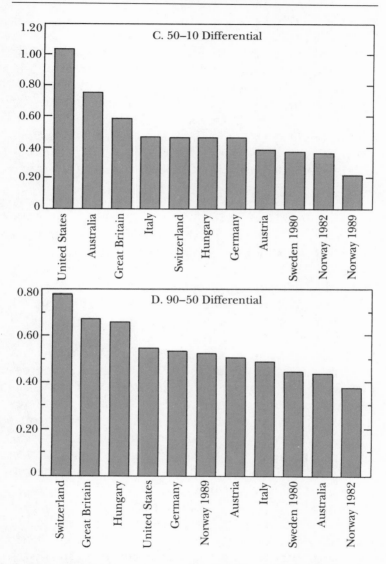

SOURCES: Adapted from *International Social Survey Programme,
1985–89; Income Distribution Survey, 1986; Class Structure and
Class Consciousness Data File, 1980, 1982; Bank of Italy Survey,*
1987.

experience, and other measures of skills. We conclude that measured characteristics help explain some of the international differences. In effect, workers in the United States at the lowest 10 percent of the wage distribution are relatively less skilled compared with workers at the middle and the top of the scale than is the case in the other countries. Put another way, a larger gap in skills in the United States accounts for more of the wage gap between those at the middle and the bottom of the wage scale in the United States than elsewhere—but it accounts for less than half of the typical difference between the United States and the other countries.

Second, we assess the contribution of labor market institutions—for example, the degree of unionization and the patterns of wage setting—to explaining the differences in wage inequality. The United States has a largely nonunion labor market with very decentralized wage setting, even in the union sector. The other countries in our sample have considerably higher rates of unionization, and most of these countries also have much more centralized wage-setting processes than those in the U.S. union sector. Further, in several countries, the terms of collective bargaining agreements are routinely extended to cover nonunion workers, and the larger union sectors in these countries may induce greater voluntary emulation of the union wage structure by the nonunion sector. Finally, the government or the union movement in some of the countries has followed explicit policies to raise the relative pay of the lowest-paid workers.

Consideration of labor market institutions thus suggests less labor market inequality in these other countries than exists in the United States, and it also implies greater compression at the bottom of the distribution than at the top. This is, of course, consistent with the pattern of inequality that we identify empirically. Moreover, the nature of union and nonunion patterns of inequality reveals interesting features of the differences between the United States and other countries with respect to the impact of labor market institutions. Specifically, our results imply that union pay policies which bring up the bottom of the union wage distribution are common to all countries, including the United States. Unions in other countries, however, appear to be more successful than U.S. unions are both in reducing inequality in the union sector and in extending such policies to the nonunion sector. It is very clear that differences in labor market institutions play a key role in explaining wage inequality.

Third, we examine international differences in the supply of and demand for labor market skills as an alternative explanation for the observed differences in inequality between the United States and other countries. We find that market forces, as best we can measure them, do not appear to be a viable explanation for the international differences in wage inequality. This finding further increases our confidence that labor market institutions are at the heart of the matter.

Finally, we present two additional pieces of empirical evidence suggesting that wage-setting institutions are an important determinant of international differences in wage distributions. First, examining the impact of centralization across the countries in our sample, we find that the degree of wage centralization, as commonly measured by comparative industrial relations researchers, is negatively associated with overall wage dispersion, the 50–10 differential in the log of wages, and the pay gap between workers with middle and low skills. That is, the more centralization, the less wage inequality. Second, as would be expected on the basis of employer responses to de facto high-wage floors, we generally find, where data are available, that those with low skills have a higher employment-to-population ratio relative to those with higher skills in the United States than elsewhere. Put simply, the low-skilled appear to have an easier time finding a job in the United States—partly, no doubt, *because* their wages are low.

This finding raises the possibility that the current very high levels of unemployment across Western Europe may be due in part to high relative wages for unskilled workers. In the 1970s, however, European unemployment rates were generally much lower than those in the United States, although the wage-setting systems in these countries were still much more centralized and there was much more union coverage than in the United States. Thus, the connection between a country's overall unemployment rate and its wage-setting institutions appears to be complicated. It is possible, however, that the highly administered wage systems in Europe reduced the ability of the labor market to adjust to the dislocations of the late 1970s and 1980s, whereas the more flexible U.S. system accommodated this adjustment to a greater extent.

This study is organized as follows. In the section "Skills and Institutions as Determinants of Wage Inequality," we explain in general terms how international differences in the variation of skills across workers and in labor market institutions influence the extent of international differences in wage inequality. We particularly emphasize why labor market institutions in the United States are likely to raise inequality here relative to the other countries in our sample. In "An Overview of International Differences in Labor Market Institutions," we briefly review the institutional arrangements governing wage determination in the other countries in our sample and compare them with the United States. In "Results," we describe the results from our decomposition of the differences in wage inequality between the United States and other countries into the causes discussed above. In "Conclusions," we summarize our results and discuss their implications.

Skills and Institutions as Determinants of Wage Inequality

Wage inequality as measured by overall wage variation or by the wage gap between workers at different parts of the distribution (for example, at the tenth versus the fiftieth percentile) is affected by the distribution of skills, both measured and unmeasured, and by the prices determined for those skills in the labor market. This price structure may include rents (extra-high wages) received by individuals employed in certain favored sectors. Labor market prices (that is, wages), in turn, are influenced by both market and institutional forces.

Market forces determine prices for skills through the interaction of the supply and demand for skills. Suppose that workers at different skill levels (for example, high school-educated versus college-educated workers) are imperfect substitutes in production. Then differences in the relative supply of or demand for skills will produce differences in relative wages across countries.[8] For example, final demand for output in one country may favor industries that (worldwide) disproportionately employ highly skilled workers. Thus, the relative demand for skilled workers in that country will be higher than it is elsewhere; and, all else being equal, we would expect skilled workers to do relatively well even in industries not directly affected by the high level of demand.

Institutional factors include the extent of collective bargaining coverage, the scope of collective bargaining where it occurs, union pay policies, and government policy toward the labor market. From each of these perspectives, we expect the United States to have a more unequal wage structure than that of other countries.

The industrial relations system can affect general wage inequality by several routes. First, unions typically raise their members' relative wages. This effect alone could increase or decrease overall wage dispersion, depending on where union workers would have been in the wage distribution in the absence of unionism. It is the union–nonunion wage gap itself (not controlling for other wage-influencing factors), however, that is relevant in "explaining" the overall wage dispersion in a descriptive sense. All else being equal, the larger this gap, however it comes about, the larger the country's general wage variance will be. Our data show that this gap is much higher in the United States than in other countries.[9] The data also indicate, however, that this factor explains only a small part of the higher inequality in the United States (on average, only 2 percent of the difference in the variance in the log of wages in the United States and that of other countries).

A second route through which the industrial relations system can affect overall wage inequality is as follows. Unions typically negotiate contracts that allow for less variation in pay than that occurring in the nonunion sector. Because unions are much less prevalent in the United States than elsewhere, the lower union variance in pay would have a smaller weight in affecting the U.S. wage dispersion than on that of other countries. Hence, we would expect a higher overall variance in wages in the United States, even if the variance of wages *within* the union and nonunion sectors were identical across countries. We find, however, that this factor explains only a small part of the difference between wage inequality in the United States and other countries (on average, about 12 percent of the difference).

The fact is that wage variation is higher in the United States than elsewhere *both in the union sector and in the nonunion sector*. This higher wage variation within each sector constitutes a third route by which the

U.S. industrial relations system raises wage inequality relative to other countries. This factor is more important than the others, explaining, on average, 86 percent of the difference in log wage variance between the United States and the other countries. To understand why wage variation is larger in both the union and the nonunion sectors in the United States, we may look to the wage-setting institutions within each sector.

With respect to the union sector, collective bargaining in the United States is relatively decentralized, with an emphasis on single-firm agreements. In most cases, these are not industrywide. By contrast, as described in greater detail below, in most of the other countries in our sample, bargaining is conducted on an industrywide or even an economywide level, as in the Scandinavian countries. Thus, there appears to be more scope for interfirm and interindustry wage differentials in the U.S. union sector than there is in the union sectors of other countries. A substantial portion of the wage inequality that we observe in the United States is associated with such firm or industry wage effects (see Davis and Haltiwanger 1991; Krueger and Summers 1988).

While a lower variance in the union sector of other countries could be achieved either by raising the bottom of the scale, restraining the top, or both, centralized bargains often emphasize the setting of wage minimums across diverse units. In Austria, Germany, Italy, Sweden, and Switzerland, for example, as well as in several European countries outside our sample, collective bargaining agreements, generally at the industry level, set minimum rates for the lowest pay group in a collective agreement. Such minimum rates, to the extent they are binding, tend to bring up the floor among workers covered by the contract. In the limiting case, a contract that covered all workers in the economy might be expected to compress the bottom of the distribution, just as a high national statutory minimum wage would. Thus, we expect to find greater compression at the bottom than at the top in the union sector in most countries compared with the union sector in the United States.

Several factors also lead us to expect more dispersion of nonunion wages in the United States than is the case elsewhere. These factors include the practice in many other countries of extending the terms of collective bargaining agreements to nonunion workers. This practice is legally mandated, for example, in Austria and Germany. These contract extensions blur the distinction between union and nonunion wage setting. To the extent that unions in all countries tend to compress wages at the bottom in the union sector, contract extension will not only reduce wage variation in the nonunion sector but will compress wages at the bottom as well. In addition, the higher degree of union organization outside the United States tends to produce more "voluntary" imitation of union pay structures by nonunion firms than it does in the United States.[10] Finally, explicit union policies and government policies in some countries aimed at bringing up the bottom of the wage distribution have further increased the impact of these factors.

In sum, wage dispersion and the degree of inequality are heavily influenced by the union sector in the foreign countries studied. This can occur through explicit mechanisms of setting wages in both the union and the nonunion sectors, through extending union wages to the nonunion sector, and through informal emulation in nonunion pay setting.

This effect of the union sector on the nonunion sector in the other countries is important. We find empirically that wage inequality, particularly the spread between the middle and the bottom of the wage distribution, is much larger in the nonunion sector of the United States than it is in other countries, whereas the difference between the union sectors in the United States and other countries is not as pronounced. This larger level of wage inequality in the U.S. nonunion sector accounts for much of the overall higher wage variation in the United States than occurs elsewhere.

International Differences
in Labor Market Institutions

In this section we provide a brief review of the institutional arrangements governing wage determination in the countries in our sample.[11] This review suggests that wage setting is indeed more decentralized in both the union and nonunion sectors in the United States than in the other countries. The American reader may discover methods and systems of wage setting abroad that are completely unfamiliar here.

Let us look first at the union sector. In our sample of countries, Sweden and Norway exhibit a very high degree of centralization of wage setting. The major union federation (abbreviated as LO here) in these countries signs an agreement with the employer association (SAF in Sweden and NHO in Norway) covering a major portion of the labor force. Collective bargaining in Austria is also very centralized, with agreements in most cases covering an entire industry or group of industries throughout the country. In Germany, contracts usually cover all employers in an industry in a state, providing a higher degree of centralization than in the United States but probably less than in Scandinavia or in Austria. And, in Italy, master industrywide agreements negotiated at the national level between unions and employer associations have traditionally been the norm.

Collective bargaining in Australia has also been characterized by considerable centralization, as the system heavily relies on government tribunals and compulsory arbitration in setting wages. It has been estimated that about 90 percent of the Australian labor force has its pay set by these tribunals. Hungary was surveyed during

the period of Communist party rule. Although most workers were in unions, wages were controlled by the state,
providing another example of centralized wage determination. For each of these countries, we would expect less
dispersion of *union* wages than there is in the United
States.

Collective bargaining in Switzerland and Britain is
less centralized than in the countries discussed above but
probably more centralized than in the United States.
While Britain, like the United States, had a mixture of
single-firm and multiemployer agreements in the 1970s,
the latest period for which quantitative data are available, bargaining appeared to be more centralized in Britain. In the United Kingdom for the years 1977–1978, 25
percent of manufacturing contracts covered more than
one firm, whereas in 1975 in the United States, only 13
percent of manufacturing contracts covered more than
one firm (see Hendricks and Kahn 1982; Deaton and
Beaumont 1980). Switzerland appears to have a mix of
centralization and decentralization. On the one hand,
many agreements in that country exclude the subject of
pay, leaving it up to individual firms. On the other hand,
there are no antitrust laws, and parties are encouraged to
form associations, leaving open the possibility of de facto
centralization. Further, it has been estimated that about
half of the work force in the private sector of Switzerland
is covered by industry collective bargaining agreements.

Events in the 1980s and 1990s have led to more decentralization of bargaining in many industrialized countries.[12] In Sweden and Norway, a decline in the influence
of the central employer federation–LO agreement began
in the 1980s, although by the end of the decade, some
recentralization had occurred in Norway. In Australia,
tribunal decisions have allowed more interfirm variation
in wage settlements. In Germany and Italy, bargaining
shifted in some cases from the industry level to the plant
level in the late 1980s. In Britain and the United States,

multiemployer units continued to crumble in the 1980s and 1990s.

We have no way of knowing whether decentralization has proceeded faster outside than inside the United States. Nonetheless, it appears that, with the possible exception of Britain, systems of collective bargaining remain more centralized in the other countries of our sample than they do in the United States. The latter does not have the centralizing institutions that are still in place in these other countries. And deunionization (that is, the decline in union membership and collective bargaining coverage) proceeded much more rapidly in the United States than in other countries (including Britain), providing an extreme form of decentralization.

The structure of collective bargaining thus leads us to expect more dispersion of union wages in the United States than elsewhere. A review of labor market institutions in other countries leads us to expect more dispersion of nonunion wages in the United States as well. In Australia, wage tribunals set minimum pay rates across both the union and nonunion sectors, whereas in then-Communist Hungary, wages in both sectors were controlled by the state. In Germany, Austria, Italy, and Switzerland, the government routinely extends the terms of collective bargaining agreements to nonunion workers.[13] It has been estimated that as of 1992, legally binding agreements at the industry level or sectoral level covered 90 percent of workers in Germany, 98 percent in Austria, and almost equally high percentages in Italy and Sweden. In Switzerland, in 1992, roughly 10 percent of all workers (or about 20 percent of nonunion workers) were nonunion employees whose wages had been set through contract extensions. These figures for 1992 suggest that whatever trends there have been toward decentralization in the 1980s and 1990s, wage setting remains considerably more centralized in Western Europe than it is in the United States.

Finally, in Sweden, Italy, Norway, and West Germany, there have been explicit union and government policies that would be expected to lead to strong compression at the bottom of the distribution. From 1968 to 1974, the LO in Sweden made a conscious effort to raise the relative wages of lower-paid workers. This led to a sharp fall in inequality. In Italy, the wage indexation system, the *scala mobile*, in place from 1975 to 1992, gave across-the-board lira increases in wages in response to inflation. The system was designed to reduce skilled–nonskilled pay differentials. By 1990, Italian employers claimed that accumulated indexation payments accounted for 40 percent of labor costs. Although other aspects of the pay package to some degree counteracted the leveling effects of indexation, Erickson and Ichino (1995) found that the system still had some independent effect in reducing inequality. In Norway in 1980, a special fund for wage increases for low-paid workers was established. In recent years in Germany, some unions, in an attempt to raise the floor, have succeeded in getting wage increases that were above sectoral-level increases for low-paid workers.

Results

In this section we describe our results from decomposing the differences in wage inequality shown in figure 1 into the causes discussed above: differences in measured skill and other characteristics between the labor forces of the different countries, the effect of unionization and patterns of wage setting, and differences in the supply of and demand for various skill levels. The full analysis of the degree of wage variance and the relative importance of each factor necessarily includes several somewhat complex equations and other mathematical techniques. The interested reader can find a full account of the methodology used as well as the results in our longer paper (Blau and Kahn 1996a).

We compiled microdata on individuals primarily in the middle to late 1980s from several sources to examine international differences in male wage inequality. (The sources are described in detail in the data appendix.) For each country, compared with the United States, it is possible to measure the relative importance of the various causes of the much larger 50–10 wage gap in the United States (the difference between wages at the fiftieth and tenth percentiles). Is it explained by the fact that there is a larger gap in the United States in skills and other measured characteristics between workers in the middle and those at the bottom of the wage scale? Or is it because of differences in the wage-setting institutions in the countries—their degree of unionization, centralization of wage bargaining, and spread of union wage floors to the non-union sector? Or is it due to differences in the demand and supply of skills?

Our first task, then, was to decompose the differences in wage inequality for the United States and each other country into two portions: that attributable to heterogeneity of the labor force and that attributable to different rewards to skill or to being employed in favored sectors of the economy. We use a technique devised by Juhn, Murphy, and Pierce (1993) for the purpose of analyzing changes in U.S. inequality. Our most interesting findings concern the causes of the higher 50–10 log wage gap in the United States. We find that, on average, about 36 percent of the higher 50–10 gap in the United States is due to this country's more diverse labor force (primarily with respect to education and experience levels). A potential explanation for the remaining 64 percent would include higher rewards for skills and being in favored sectors in the economy in the United States than elsewhere. What we have called labor market prices are thus extremely important in explaining why the United States has such a large pay gap between workers at the middle and those at the bottom of the distribution.

We also find that prices widen the 90–50 gap in the United States, but to a much smaller degree than they affect the 50–10 gap. This difference is perhaps accounted for by the frequent practice in European collective bargaining of negotiating a single-industry minimum wage but not specifying wages for those at the top. It is worth noting, however, that personal characteristics actually narrow the 90–50 gap in the United States relative to that elsewhere. Thus, in the United States, those at the middle, compared with middle-earners in other countries, are well qualified relative to both those at the bottom and those at the top. This may reflect the far greater likelihood of college attendance among middle-wage earners in the United States.

This analysis has established that labor market prices are a major cause of higher inequality in the United States, particularly with respect to the very low relative wages at the bottom of the distribution. This pattern is consistent with the institutional information we discussed earlier on collective bargaining. It is possible, however, that the larger wage gap in the United States could be attributable to a larger supply of low-skill workers in the United States relative to the demand for them.

To examine this question, we constructed three skill groups ("high," "middle," and "low") in each country, on the basis of workers' education and experience levels. We then created indexes of the relative supply of and demand for workers of each skill level in each country. The supply indexes measure the share of the work force that each skill group comprises. The demand indexes tell the degree to which the industrial-occupational structure of a given country favors workers of various skill levels. For example, a country with a large service sector would have a high relative demand for the kinds of workers who are typically employed in services.

What we found is that low-skill workers are actually *scarcer* relative to demand in the United States than they are in the other countries in the sample. This result would imply that low-skill workers should do better relative to others in the United States than they do in the other countries. We find the exact opposite pattern in the data, however. Supply and demand therefore cannot explain these results.

Although supply and demand do not appear to be viable explanations for the poor showing of low-skill employed workers in the United States, our discussion of wage-setting institutions is consistent with the wage patterns. Collective bargaining covers a far larger share of the work force in other countries than it does in the United States, and unions outside the United States have especially large effects in raising the wages of unskilled union workers and of extending these wage increases to nonunion workers. In fact, looking across all the countries in our sample, we find support for the idea that centralized wage setting in general raises the relative wages of those at the bottom of the wage distribution.

Industrial relations researchers have devised rankings of the OECD countries with respect to the degree of centralization in their wage-setting institutions. Not surprisingly, the United States ranks as the country with the least centralized wage-setting institutions, and Austria and the Scandinavian countries rank among those with the most centralized. We find a statistically significant negative correlation between a country's ranking with respect to centralization and its overall level of wage dispersion. That is, the greater the degree of centralization in wage setting, the smaller the level of wage inequality. This finding appears to be driven by greater compression at the bottom of the wage distribution in countries with more centralized wage setting: the 50–10 log wage gap—that is, the wage differential between workers at the fiftieth percentile and at the tenth percentile of the wage distribution—as well as the wage differential between middle-skill and low-skill workers, is also significantly negatively related to the degree of wage centralization. This suggests that our findings for individual "two by two" comparisons of the United States with other countries represent a more general phenomenon in the industrialized world.

We believe that the decentralized wage-setting system in the United States results in relatively low wages for less-skilled workers. If it is indeed the case that the centralized wage-setting institutions of other countries are responsible for the higher relative wages of less-skilled workers in the other industrialized countries, the economics of labor demand predicts that employers outside the United States would demand a smaller relative quantity of low-skill workers, all else being equal, as a result of high administered wages.

To examine whether this hypothesis is true, we measured the employment-to-population ratio (that is, the likelihood that someone has a job) for each of the skill groups in the countries for which we had the data. (This is a considerably smaller group of countries than those for which we have wage information.) We found in every country that middle-skill workers were more likely to be employed than were low-skill workers. But the gap was much larger in Germany, Austria, and Norway than in the United States: in these countries, people with low skills were much less likely, relative to those with middle skills, to find work than were low-skilled workers in the United States. This finding suggests a disemployment effect of the high wages for the low skilled in these countries. The employment gap between low- and middle-skill workers, however, was about the same in Australia as in the United States, and actually smaller in Britain than in the United States. Thus, the finding of an adverse employment effect is not universal in our data. Among those countries for which information on employment rates is available, however, it does hold for the countries in which there was the most wage compression between middle- and low-skill workers (Germany, Austria, and Norway).

Conclusions

In this study we compare male wage inequality in the United States and nine other industrialized countries, primarily in the middle to late 1980s. Consistent with previous work, the results indicate that overall wage inequality is much greater in the United States than elsewhere. It is noteworthy, however, that when we disaggregate the measure of inequality to examine various parts of the wage distribution, we find that the distribution in other countries is much more compressed at the bottom relative to the United States than at the top. Thus, while the differential between the wage at the fiftieth percentile of the wage distribution and at the tenth percentile is considerably larger in the United States than elsewhere, the U.S. wage differential between the ninetieth and the fiftieth percentiles is only slightly larger than in the other countries.

We evaluate several possible explanations for these patterns. First, differences in the distribution of measured characteristics (such as education levels) across countries were found to be responsible for some but not all of the international differences in wage distribution. Even if the United States had other countries' distribution of measured characteristics, its total wage variation would remain much higher than elsewhere. Moreover, while the gap between the middle and bottom portions of the U.S. wage distribution would be reduced, the high–middle gap would be increased. Most important, the wage distribution in other countries would still be more compressed at the bottom than at the top relative to the distribution in the United States. These results suggest that U.S. labor market institutions and resulting labor market prices contribute to our observed findings.

Second, we note that, unlike the United States, most of the other countries in our sample have very centralized systems of collective bargaining, and many have provisions to extend the terms of union contracts to nonunion workers. Voluntary emulation of the union wage structure by nonunion firms as a reaction to threat effects (that is, the threat of unionization if higher wages are not paid) is also likely to be greater in these other countries, given the larger size of their union sectors. Consistent with these observations, we find a larger variance of wages and less wage compression at the bottom within *both* the U.S. union and nonunion sectors compared with those sectors in other countries.

Indeed, the larger variance of wages in the United States is primarily due to the higher variance that prevails in this country *within* each of these sectors. Moreover, controlling for the distribution of measured characteristics, both of these salient features of the U.S. distribution—a higher wage variance and a greater spread at the bottom—are more pronounced in the nonunion than in the union sector. This result suggests that contract extension and other mechanisms that extend union-determined wages to the nonunion sector in other countries have a larger effect on the wage structures of these countries relative to the United States than do their more centralized wage-setting institutions within the union sector.

Third, we examine indexes of relative supplies and demands across countries to see whether market forces could provide an alternative explanation for the observed patterns, particularly for the high relative wages of low-skill workers in other countries. The results of taking both supply and demand into account suggest that low-skill workers should fare *better* relative to middle-skill workers in the United States than they do in other countries and thus that supply–demand conditions cannot explain the smaller low-to-middle-skill differentials that prevail in these countries.

Finally, we present two additional pieces of empirical evidence suggesting that wage-setting institutions are an important determinant of international differences in wage distributions: (1) Looking across countries, we find that wage centralization, as commonly measured by comparative industrial relations researchers, is negatively associated with wage dispersion, the 50–10 differential in the log of wages, and the pay gap between middle- and low-skill workers; and (2) We examine possible employment responses to the pattern of greater wage compression at the bottom of the wage distribution in other countries compared with that in the United States. As would be expected on the basis of employer responses to high wage floors, we generally find that low-skill workers have a higher employment-to-population ratio relative to the higher-skilled workers in the United States than in other countries.

To the extent that institutions are important in affecting wage inequality, we would expect adverse effects on employment and productivity as a result of resource allocation effects. We have presented some evidence that this is the case. To some degree, labor market policies such as government employment or training programs and relocation subsidies can compensate for such effects, although we did not find general evidence of disproportionate government employment among the low skilled outside the United States.

One interpretation of government labor market policy in many OECD countries is that wage-leveling policies are encouraged by governments to achieve a desired (relatively low) level of wage inequality. The greater compression at the bottom, in particular, suggests that these other countries attempt to use the labor market to provide a "safety net" for low-wage workers to a greater extent than is the case in the United States. The more activist government policies of many OECD countries regarding employment, training, and relocation may be seen in part as corrective measures for the adverse employment and allocation effects of the wage distribution policies. The current high levels of unemployment across Europe are a major cause for concern there, and proposals to make wage-setting less centralized there may be in part a response to these high unemployment rates.

Data Appendix

This study is based on microdata on individuals from each country in our sample. The data were obtained from a number of sources. First, we used the International Social Survey Programme (ISSP) for the following countries and time periods: Austria (1985 to 1987 and 1989), West Germany (1985 to 1988), Hungary (1986 to 1988), Switzerland (1987), Britain (1985 to 1989), the United States (1985 to 1989), and Norway (1989). The ISSP is an internationally cooperative effort in data collection in which, for each year in each of the participating countries, a random sample of the population is asked a series of standardized questions related to the labor market. This data source is well suited to the kind of international comparisons we carry out here.

We supplemented the ISSP with several other microdatabases in order to expand our coverage of countries. Specifically, we used the Class Structure and Class Consciousness (CSCC) database for Sweden (1980), and also for Norway (1982), since the data were available (this provided a second Norwegian data set); the Income Distribution Survey (IDS) for Australia (1986); and a Bank of Italy (BI) survey for Italy (1987).[14] In all cases, the sample is restricted to male wage and salary workers, aged eighteen to sixty-five.

We performed a special comparison for 1984 between the United States and Sweden using two addi-

27

tional databases with more detailed information on personal characteristics and earnings, the Michigan Panel Study of Income Dynamics (PSID) and the Swedish Household Market and Nonmarket Activities Survey (HUS).[15] In this portion of the analysis, the sample is further restricted to full-time workers and, in the case of the U.S. data, to whites. White males are used instead of all males in order to produce a relatively homogeneous U.S. sample to compare with the Swedish data. (The ISSP did not collect information on race.) Our results using these superior data were completely consistent with those obtained from our other sources, considerably strengthening our confidence in the findings of this study.

For all cases except the 1984 Sweden–United States comparison, the earnings variable supplied by the data source is expressed on an annual or monthly basis. We use a regression adjustment to correct these measures for differences in weekly hours worked, but in most cases do not have information on weeks worked. Thus, the numbers on which figure 1 is based should be viewed as earnings corrected for time inputs, acknowledging the data limitations. For the 1984 Sweden–United States comparison, however, we are able to directly compute hourly earnings.

Notes

1. An example of the importance of labor market inequality is provided by the U.S. experience in the 1980s, when rising wage inequality was sufficient to counteract the effects of economic expansion in reducing poverty (Blank 1993; Cutler and Katz 1991).

2. The impact of administered wages on employment is a controversial issue. For research on both sides of the issue, see Card and Krueger (1995); Card, Kramarz, and Lemieux (1994); Katz, Loveman, and Blanchflower (1995); Abowd, Kramarz, Lemieux, and Margolis (1995); Edin and Topel (1994); and Neumark and Wascher (1992).

3. See Blau and Kahn (1992; 1995; and 1996b). This difference between the United States and other countries is due to the greater compression at the bottom of the wage distribution in these other countries, which disproportionately benefits employed women (Blau and Kahn 1996b).

4. For evidence of rising inequality in several countries, see Katz, Loveman, and Blanchflower (1995); Juhn, Murphy, and Pierce (1993); Katz and Murphy (1992); Bound and Johnson (1992); Erickson and Ichino (1995); Edin and Holmlund (1995); Davis (1992); Gottschalk and Joyce (1991); and OECD (1993).

5. In Blau and Kahn (1992; 1995; and 1996b), we consider the consequences of differences in wage inequality across countries for international differences in the gender gap.

6. Among the countries in our sample for which the

OECD (1993) also has data (that is, Austria, Germany, Italy, Norway, Sweden, and the United Kingdom), the 50–10 gap averaged .59 log points higher in the United States, whereas the 90–50 gap averaged .25 log points higher. (Australia was also included in the OECD data, but only for nonsupervisory workers.) In our hours-corrected microdata for these countries, the 50–10 gap averaged .61 log points higher in the United States, whereas the 90–50 gap averaged .032 log points higher. The higher U.S. level of relative inequality at the top in the OECD data appears to reflect differences for the United States between the Current Population Survey (CPS) data that the OECD used and the International Social Survey Programme (ISSP) data that we employ. In any case, the same qualitative pattern of considerably larger differences between the United States and other countries at the bottom of the distribution than at the top emerges regardless of the data source.

7. The claim about poverty holds if we are comparing countries with similar average real wage levels, as is the case here. For example, in 1988, hourly compensation in manufacturing in the OECD countries other than the United States averaged 98 percent of the U.S. level, adjusting for exchange rates (U.S. Department of Commerce 1992, p. 841).

8. This assumes barriers to the mobility of capital, labor, and/or goods across national boundaries so that skill prices are not equalized.

9. Much of this higher U.S. union–nonunion wage differential is due to a higher U.S. union–nonunion wage gap, controlling for personal characteristics, rather than to differences in the personal characteristics of union and nonunion workers (Blanchflower and Freeman 1992). This suggests a strong causal role for the industrial relations system.

10. This will be the case if union "threat" effects dominate any negative "crowding" effects in the nonunion sector that are caused by the adverse employment effects of unionism. Kahn and Curme (1987) found for the United States that, other things being equal, nonunion wage dispersion was lower in highly unionized than in less unionized industries.

11. For information on wage-setting institutions in these countries, see Edin and Holmlund (1995); OECD (1989); Katz (1993); Tomandl and Fuerboeck (1986); Killingsworth (1990); Wrong (1987); USDOL (1992); and Treu (1990).

12. This discussion of recent trends is based on Katz (1993); Edin and Holmlund (1995); Edin and Topel (1994); and OECD (1989).

13. See Kennedy (1982), Tomandl and Fuerboeck (1986), Treu (1990), and *European Industrial Relations Review* (Oct. 1992). A sizable proportion of Italian workers are self-employed or work in an underground or informal sector in which government-mandated benefits are not paid. The self-employed are not included in our analysis because of our interest in the wage determination process for wage and salary workers. Further, it is likely that since employment in the informal sector is illegal, it is underreported by the respondents in our survey-based data. Thus, we may understate wage inequality in Italy.

14. For descriptions of these data, see Blanchflower and Freeman (1992)—ISSP; Rosenfeld and Kalleberg (1990)—CSCC; Blackburn and Bloom (1991)—IDS; and Erickson and Ichino (1995)—BI. The ISSP had information on Italy, but it did not collect data on the respondents' industrial sector; we therefore used the BI data instead. Further, preliminary results indicated that the Australian data in the ISSP were inconsistent with those of other sources, leading us to use the more consistent IDS data.

15. For a description of the PSID, see Blau and Kahn (forthcoming), and for information on the HUS, see Edin and Holmlund (1995).

References

Abowd, John, Francis Kramarz, Thomas Lemieux, and David Margolis. "Minimum Wages and Youth Unemployment in France and the US." Paper presented at the NBER Summer Institute, July 1995.

Blackburn, McKinley L., and David E. Bloom. "Changes in the Structure of Family Income Inequality in the U.S. and Other Industrialized Nations during the 1980s." Manuscript. New York: Columbia University, June 1991.

Blanchflower, David, and Richard Freeman. "Unionism in the U.S. and Other Advanced O.E.C.D. Countries." *Industrial Relations* 31 (Winter 1992): 56–79.

Blank, Rebecca. "Why Were Poverty Rates So High in the 1980s?" In *Poverty and Prosperity in the USA in the Late Twentieth Century*, edited by Dimitri Papadimitriou and Edward Wolff. London: MacMillan Press, 1993.

Blau, Francine D., and Lawrence M. Kahn. "The Gender Earnings Gap: Learning from International Comparisons." *American Economic Review* 82 (May 1992): 533–38.

———. "The Gender Earnings Gap: Some International Evidence." In *Differences and Changes in Wage Structures*, edited by Richard Freeman and Lawrence Katz. Chicago, Ill.: University of Chicago Press, 1995.

———. "International Differences in Male Wage Inequality:

Institutions versus Market Forces." Cambridge, Mass.: NBER Working Paper no. 4678, March 1994; *Journal of Political Economy* 104 (August 1996a): 791–837.

———. "Wage Structure and Gender Earnings Differentials: An International Comparison." *Economica* 63 (May 1996b supplement): S29–S62.

———. "Swimming Upstream: Trends in the Gender Wage Differential in the 1980s." *Journal of Labor Economics* (forthcoming).

Bound, John, and George Johnson. "Changes in the Structure of Wages in the 1980's: An Evaluation of Alternative Explanations." *American Economic Review* 82 (June 1992): 371–92.

Card, David, and Alan B. Krueger. *Myth and Measurement: The New Economics of the Minimum Wage.* Princeton, N.J.: Princeton University Press, 1995.

Card, David, Francis Kramarz, and Thomas Lemieux. "Changes in the Relative Structure of Wages and Employment: A Comparison of the United States, Canada, and France." Manuscript. Princeton, N.J.: Princeton University, December 1994.

Cutler, David M., and Lawrence F. Katz. "Macroeconomic Performance and the Disadvantaged." *Brookings Papers on Economic Activity* 1991: 1–74.

Davis, Steven J. "Cross-Country Patterns of Change in Relative Wages." Cambridge, Mass.: NBER Working Paper no. 4085, June 1992.

Davis, Steven J., and John Haltiwanger. "Wage Dispersion between and within U.S. Manufacturing Plants." *Brookings Papers on Economic Activity: Microeconomics* 1991: 115–80.

Deaton, D. R., and P. B. Beaumont. "The Determinants of Bargaining Structure: Some Large Scale Survey Evidence for Britain." *British Journal of Industrial Relations* 18 (July 1980): 202–16.

Edin, Per-Anders, and Bertil Holmlund. "The Swedish Wage Structure: The Rise and Fall of Solidarity Wage Policy." In *Differences and Changes in Wage Structures*, edited by Richard Freeman and Lawrence Katz. Chicago, Ill.: University of Chicago Press, 1995.

Edin, Per-Anders, and Robert Topel. "Wage Policy and Restructuring: The Swedish Labor Market since 1960." Manuscript. Chicago: University of Chicago. December 1994.

Erickson, Chris, and Andrea Ichino. "Wage Differentials in Italy: Market Forces and Institutions." In *Differences and Changes in Wage Structures*, edited by Richard Freeman and Lawrence Katz. Chicago, Ill.: University of Chicago Press, 1995.

European Industrial Relations Review (EIRR). "Minimum Pay in 18 Countries." No. 225 (October 1992): 14–21.

Gottschalk, Peter, and Mary Joyce. "Changes in Earnings Inequality: An International Perspective." Manuscript. Boston: Boston College, 1991.

Hendricks, Wallace E., and Lawrence M. Kahn. "The Determinants of Bargaining Structure in U.S. Manufacturing Industries." *Industrial and Labor Relations Review* 35 (January 1982): 181–95.

Juhn, Chinhui, Kevin M. Murphy, and Brooks Pierce. "Accounting for the Slowdown in Black-White Wage Convergence." In *Workers and Their Wages*, edited by M. Kosters. Washington, D.C.: AEI Press, 1991.

———. "Wage Inequality and the Rise in Returns to Skill." *Journal of Political Economy* 101 (June 1993): 410–44.

Kahn, Lawrence M., and Michael Curme. "Unions and Nonunion Wage Dispersion." *Review of Economics and Statistics* 69 (November 1987): 600–607.

Katz, Harry C. "The Decentralization of Collective Bargaining: A Literature Review and Comparative Analysis." *Industrial and Labor Relations Review* 47 (October 1993): 3–22.

Katz, Lawrence F., and Kevin M. Murphy. "Changes in Relative Wages, 1963–87: Supply and Demand Factors." *Quarterly Journal of Economics,* 107 (February 1992): 35–78.

Katz, Lawrence F., Gary W. Loveman, and David Blanchflower. "A Comparison of Changes in the Structure of Wages in Four OECD Countries." In *Differences and Changes in Wage Structures*, edited by Richard Freeman and Lawrence Katz. Chicago, Ill.: University of Chicago Press, 1995.

Kennedy, Thomas. *European Labor Relations.* Lexington, Mass.: D. C. Heath, 1982.

Killingsworth, Mark. *The Economics of Comparable Worth.* Kalamazoo, Mich.: W. E. Upjohn Institute for Employment Research, 1990.

Krueger, Alan, and Lawrence Summers. "Efficiency Wages and the Inter-Industry Wage Structure." *Econometrica* 56 (March 1988): 259–93.

Neumark, David, and William Wascher. "Employment Effects of Minimum and Subminimum Wages: Panel Data on State Minimum Wage Laws." *Industrial and Labor Relations Review* 46 (October 1992): 55–81.

OECD. *Employment Outlook: July 1993.* Paris: OECD, 1993.

———. *OECD Economic Surveys: Norway 1988/1989.* Paris: OECD, 1989.

Rosenfeld, Rachel, and Arne Kalleberg. "A Cross-national Comparison of the Gender Gap in Income." *American Journal of Sociology* 96 (July 1990): 69–106.

Tomandl, Theodor, and Karl Fuerboeck. *Social Partnership.* Ithaca, N.Y.: ILR Press, 1986.

Treu, T. "Italy." *Bulletin of Comparative Labour Relations* 19 (1990): 227–50.

U.S. Department of Commerce. *Statistical Abstract of the United States 1992.* Washington, D.C.: U.S. Government Printing Office, 1992.

U.S. Department of Labor (USDOL). *Foreign Labor Trends: Hungary 1991–2.* Washington, D.C.: U.S. Government Printing Office, 1992.

Wrong, Gale. "Switzerland." *Bulletin of Comparative Labour Relations* 16 (1987): 183–201.

About the Authors

FRANCINE D. BLAU is the Frances Perkins Professor of Industrial and Labor Relations at Cornell University, where she also serves as research director and codirector of the Institute for Labor Market Policies in the School of Industrial and Labor Relations. She is a research associate at the National Bureau of Economic Research and an associate editor of the *Journal of Economic Perspectives*. She is a former vice president of the American Economic Association and is currently president-elect of the Industrial Relations Research Association. She has lectured or taught at the University of Illinois at Urbana-Champaign, the Australian National University, Trinity College, and Yale University. She is the author of numerous books and articles, including *The Economics of Women, Men, and Work,* with Marianne A. Ferber (2d ed., 1992); "Rising Wage Inequality and the U.S. Gender Gap," with Lawrence M. Kahn, in the *American Economic Review* (1994); and "Wage Structure and Gender Earnings Differentials: An International Comparison," with Lawrence M. Kahn, in *Economica* (1996).

LAWRENCE M. KAHN is professor of labor economics and collective bargaining in the New York State School of Industrial and Labor Relations at Cornell University. He is an associate editor of *Industrial and Labor Relations Review* and a member of the American Economic Association and of the Industrial Relations Research Association.

He previously taught at the Australian National University and the University of Illinois at Urbana-Champaign. His fields of specialization include labor economics, econometrics, and discrimination, and he has written several books and articles, including *Economics of the Employment Relationship,* with Robert Flanagan, Robert Smith, and Ronald Ehrenberg (1989); "International Differences in Male Wage Inequality: Institutions versus Market Forces," with Francine D. Blau, in the *Journal of Political Economy* (1996); and "Swimming Upstream: Trends in the Gender Wage Differential in the 1980s," with Francine D. Blau, in the *Journal of Labor Economics* (forthcoming).

AEI STUDIES ON UNDERSTANDING
ECONOMIC INEQUALITY
Marvin H. Kosters, series editor

THE DISTRIBUTION OF WEALTH: INCREASING INEQUALITY?
John C. Weicher

EARNINGS INEQUALITY: THE INFLUENCE OF CHANGING
OPPORTUNITIES AND CHOICES
Robert H. Haveman

RELATIVE WAGE TRENDS, WOMEN'S WORK, AND
FAMILY INCOME
Chinhui Juhn

WAGE INEQUALITY: INTERNATIONAL COMPARISONS OF
ITS SOURCES
Francine D. Blau and Lawrence M. Kahn